In 1979, Leonard Jacobson moved to Paris to become a writer. Over the next ten years, he lived in France, Spain, Mexico, Thailand, and Australia and wrote two books, including *Lost in Mexico: Journey into an Exotic Land*. He then moved to Seattle, Washington, and began a new life as a Counselor, Child Therapist, and a twenty-year career as a High School Wrestling Coach. More recently, he spent five years living and working in a church as a Building Manager and Sexton/Custodian. He currently lives in Vancouver, Washington, and works for the Veterans Administration in Community Care.

To my son, Max.

Leonard Jacobson

LOST IN MEXICO: JOURNEY INTO AN EXOTIC LAND

AUSTIN MACAULEY PUBLISHERS™

LONDON • CAMBRIDGE • NEW YORK • SHARJAH

Ordering Information
Quantity sales: Special discounts are available on quantity purchases by corporations, associations, and others. For details, contact the publisher at the address below.

Publisher's Cataloguing-in-Publication data
Jacobson, Leonard
Lost in Mexico: Journey Into an Exotic Land

ISBN 9781643787565 (Paperback)
ISBN 9781647505080 (ePub e-book)

Library of Congress Control Number: 2022904892

www.austinmacauley.com/us

First Published 2023
Austin Macauley Publishers LLC
40 Wall Street, 33rd Floor, Suite 3302
New York, NY 10005
USA

mail-usa@austinmacauley.com
+1 (646) 5125767

To all my friends and family, who have supported my quest for all these many years.

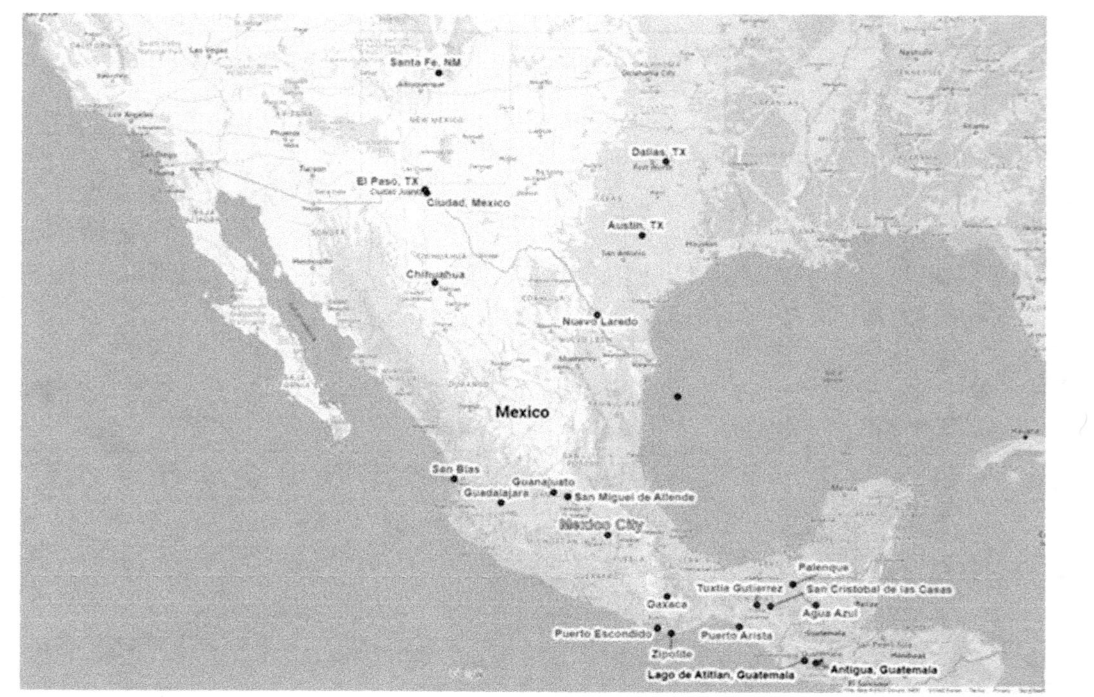

Santa Fe, NM
Dallas, TX
El Paso, TX
Ciudad, Mexico
Austin, TX
Chihuahua
Nuevo Laredo
Mexico
San Blas
Guanajuato
Guadalajara
San Miguel de Allende
Mexico City
Palenque
Tuxtla Gutierrez
San Cristobal de las Casas
Oaxaca
Agua Azul
Puerto Escondido
Puerto Arista
Zipolite
Lago de Atitlan, Guatemala
Antigua, Guatemala

I entered Mexico through Juarez, a dirty, crowded border town on the other side of El Paso, Texas. A flight from Albuquerque to Dallas. Another from Dallas to El Paso. Then not wanting to know what I was getting myself into, I grabbed my bags and caught a taxi to Juarez. The driver was a large Mexican with a pot belly and three-day beard with an old, beat-up cab with a patchwork paint job. He said he could take me to Juarez for twenty dollars. I climbed in and was on my way.

I remember going over the bridge. Mexicans walking to and from El Paso. Being dropped off on the main drag of Juarez and how unbelievably squalid it looked. It was a hot Sunday in early November and the street life was winding down with late afternoon tourists, drunk servicemen and locals as I looked for a cheap room for the night. I knew I had entered someplace less certain, less predictable, more confronting than where I left. And as I walked down the street with the sun bearing down on me and foreign sounds in my ear, I wondered why I had put myself in such a position.

****

A day later I am between two railroad cars looking over the Copper Canyon. It is three times larger than the Grand Canyon and for hours we have been passing through it. The sun is setting and a cool breeze passes over me. Green cascades the walls of the canyon and every fifteen minutes or so, a waterfall comes into view. Occasionally, a Mexican will see me and wave to me and I will wave back. My eyes tear up as I look out.

****

The next day I am in Chihuahua: a hot, dry, dusty industrial city in Northern Mexico. It's the kind of place you would never go except to catch a bus for someplace else, which is why I am here. My bus leaves for San Blas, my destination in the morning.

I must admit, you get a good feed in Chihuahua: soup, salad, chicken, rice and beans, vegetables, tortillas, dessert and coffee all for three hundred pesos, about two dollars. Beer, stronger and thicker than in the States, is sixty cents a bottle. I leave the restaurant stuffed and a little drunk. The sun is hot and I look for shade as I walk toward my hotel, a cheap place two blocks from the bus station I found for four hundred pesos a night.

When I get to my room, I collapse on the bed. My mind drifts to Santa Fe, the woman I left behind, our trip to India, a reality until a month ago. The memories are too painful and I think of the book I have come to Mexico to write. I see the opening pages in front of me, the words are alive and writing themselves out, until I fall asleep, exhausted, my mind filled with fantastic visions of what is to come.

****

The next day, I am San Blas and within hours I know it's a bust. For one thing, it's too hot and humid and bugs are everywhere and it's not even summer. Also, it's expensive. The cheapest place I could find was eight hundred pesos a night and the restaurants are overpriced. Wherever you go, riffraff, con-men, drifters, drug dealers, drunks, travelers who have run out of money, all trying to put the bite on you. The locals aren't particularly friendly, either. It seems like they don't even want tourists there.

I spend the next two days getting drunk and stoned, talking to other travelers, and trying to keep an arm's length away from the riffraff. On the morning of the third day, I catch a bus for the next big city: Guadalajara.

****

At the fights in Guadalajara. Ringside seats where you literally dodge flying blood. The crowd is wild behind me. The boxing is Mexican style: the boxers never taking a step backward, blocking punches with their faces, until one falls in a bloody heap. A moment later, the fighters embrace and the crowd roars its approval. Two new fighters enter the ring and it starts all over again.

Guadalajara. It sounds pretty, like sweet smelling flowers in a warm breeze. The reality is being dragged along wide avenues by a throng of poor, brown skinned people in a stifling heat. Pollution hangs heavy in the air, choking your breath as car horns blare in a deafening madness. It is

11

everything you imagined a Third World city to be, except you are there, the latest destination in this already wayward adventure. I stop by the side of the street for a drink and the crowd moves on. A suspicious looking liquid is poured into a plastic bag and given to me. Sweating, my throat parched, my body covered with bed-bug bites, I look up into a yellow sky and say, "THIS IS NOT HAPPENING!"

****

On an airplane from Guadalajara to Oaxaca, a place I did not know existed two days ago. The plane is immaculate. Mexican airline stewardesses in starched uniforms smelling of perfume, handing out technicolor food wrapped in cellophane. It all seems surreal after the last week. I half expect to see three dirty faced, barefoot Mexican boys running down the aisle shouting *"Empanadas!" "Refrescos!" "Pan Dulces!"* I shake my head and laugh at my predicament.

****

Oaxaca: the capital city of the state of Oaxaca and one of the handful of states making up Southern Mexico. You can feel the difference. The land is higher, greener, cooler, stiller. I have been here the last two days, the fifth Mexican city I have slept in, in eight days. In a week, I have travelled from the top of Mexico to almost the bottom, a haphazard adventure on buses and trains and planes and taxis. Will this be the one?

The days are bright and hot and the nights almost cold in Oaxaca, the town a bustling little metropolis set seven thousand feet high in the Mexican mountains. It could do. A big plaza surrounded by cafes and restaurants and where music is played at night. The day before going out with a Pakistani photographer I met while visiting the Ruins. Getting drunk on mescal and falling asleep in the afternoon on a crowded bus.

Later, at a cafe by the plaza, distracted by the voices of tourists, I consider the possibility of living here, what my life would be like. I am going to move on.

****

It is my third day in Puerto Escondido and I can no longer pretend, I am lost. Days spent playing in the ocean and gazing endlessly into a blue green sea under thatched roofed cafes set in sand. One day I will find a place to settle down and get stuck into the book, but until then, I should make the best of my circumstances, shouldn't I?

This Mexico can be a dangerous place. Yesterday, I took a walk along the beach and stopped to swim in a cove between two large rocks. The water was turbulent, like a whirlpool and before I knew what was happening, I was dragged out into the ocean. Waves crashed on top of me from all different directions, pulling me further out where my feet could no longer touch the bottom. I tried to swim back in, but the undertow was too great and for twenty minutes I thrashed desperately to get back to shore. Finally,

I don't know exactly how, I made it back to the sand and collapsed.

But mostly, I eat shrimp and drink beer and smoke weed and walk the streets in the town at night.

****

Time to split Puerto Escondido. Enough time spent on the old R & R besides this place is getting dangerous. Just a few hours ago, I was in the middle of a crazy surf brawl. We were in the disco, dancing away, when my friend, the local surf hero, was attacked by a couple of guys. I grabbed one guy and someone punched me and the next thing I knew, chairs started flying and everyone went for the doors.

When we got outside, it became a fight between the local surfers from Puerto Escondido and the surfers from Acapulco. The home team took a beating. There was one Acapulco surfer who was about six feet tall and was taking on all comers. He gave my little friend a thrashing and I was tempted to give it a shot, but John, my English friend, pulled me away. The guy was hardly a giant, though there was no way I was going to win a fight under the circumstances and we took off in the other direction. It was a shame, because I was doing well with a fine, young senorita from Acapulco.

****

Under warm woolen blankets in San Cristobal Las Casas, I don't even understand anymore. Two days ago, I was roasting my balls off in Puerto Escondido. Then after travelling across and down on buses all day and night, I end up shivering under a pile of blankets. I left with my friend John, who persuaded me San Cristobal Las Casas was the place to go. It didn't take much convincing, though I was thinking of giving the mountain cities of middle Mexico a try. There is a place called San Miguel de Allende, a famous artist town I have I have been resisting in the hopes of finding some other undiscovered jewel in the Mexican landscape.

We came into San Cristobal on an old bus early in the morning. The bus was packed as we inched up the mountains, the engine groaning and wheezing. An old Indian was leaning against me asleep, his brown hands swollen and cracked. Everyone else on the bus except for John and I were Indian and most of them were awake, looking out the windows amazed, their brown eyes gleaming. As we rose higher and higher, the cold set in and you could see small white clouds of condensed breath throughout the bus. An enormous brown bird, flew beside the bus, flapping its giant wings. Finally, as the sun peeked over the mountains, we came to San Cristobal.

San Cristobal is *beautiful*. Cobblestone streets and whitewashed buildings set high in green mountains. Walking the streets in the fog the last two days, you are in another world. The food is great: thick, homemade bread and fresh fruit and vegetables for almost nothing. This bowl of vegetable soup I had was a work of art. You felt like you could conquer the world after eating it, but I'm not freezing my ass off for a bowl of soup. We leave for Guatemala in the morning. John says it's not to be missed.

****

Another search and passport check. Every ten or fifteen miles the bus stops, we all get off the bus and have our papers checked and sometimes, we are searched as well. Once is an eerie feeling, but after the fourth time in an hour you start to wonder what you're getting yourself into. Soldiers, barely eighteen years old, come up to you with a rifle in their hands like it's their brand-new toy. Many of them aren't even in uniform. I usually speak a little Spanish and they are friendly enough. Most of them don't want to go through this shit any more than we do. It makes sense when you think we are getting close to Nicaragua and El Salvador.

Guatemala is different from Mexico, the landscape wilder and more tropical. Last night as the sun was setting, we came from above and descended into thick, green bush. From orange and green, we went to dark green and then, black, until we were surrounded by darkness and the noises and smell of the jungle. We stopped for the night in a small town and looked for a place to stay. We found a pension that charged us seventy-five cents a night and had a menu of black beans, eggs and tortillas. The tortillas were big and thick like pizza crusts and a woman put them in front of us as soon as we sat down. So, we had eggs, black beans, tortillas and Nescafe with whisky.

****

For a week, I have been in Lago de Atitlan and I need to make a decision to stay or not. You would think I would have given up my sense urgency and enjoy myself like any self-respecting Puerto Rican. The problem is: *that is the problem*. Enjoy, fuck around, be open to my pleasures, these are not diversions, this *is* my life.

John, my English friend who is travelling the world before he begins his law career in four months, looked at me in horror when I told him I was going to be thirty in a couple of months. *The Parents. What Must the Parents Think?* Such questions are no longer central to my motivations. ...Though every once in a while, I do wonder what the parents are thinking.

Ah, but Lake Atitlan is so very beautiful. It is not right to categorize these things, but have I ever been anywhere more breathtaking than this place? Let me describe it for you:

Lago de Atitlan is set in green mountains surrounded by volcanoes. In the middle is a lake, but unlike any lake you have ever seen. It changes colors and has waves they call the "*Chocomil*" and it is alive and moody and full of spirit. The sky, too, is different, part of the earth and not some removed and distant thing. Sunny and bright days and cool nights with thousands of stars just out of reach. The local Indians wear colors you would imagine in a hallucinogenic drug trip. Wonderful, ornate, spectacularly colored garments worn with pride and relish and everywhere you look in Lago de Atitlan they are there, like tropical birds with their omniscient smiles and giggles.

Yesterday, I got stoned with my friends Gabby and Josan and drove outside town in their little Volkswagen. They took me to their spot and all I could do was stand back open-mouthed, overwhelmed by what was in front of me. The Sun was setting, putting shadows and silver beams on the Lake, the volcanos regal in the distance. Green mountains on each side and behind, rising to the sky, thick and green, like a lush blanket encircling us. A changing rainbow of colors, one hue after another, splashed across the sky. I could not be sure what was in front of me was real, or some magnificent painting thrown up before my eyes. I stood there is awe, half believing, stunned by the beauty, trying to make sense of it all.

****

On the bus from Guatemala back to Mexico. I could have stayed in Lake Atitlan. Josan and Gabby said they could find me a place to stay for not too much money. Wealthy Venezuelans of Trinidadian descent, they lived in a big house by the Lake with walls and guard dogs, while their parents lived in Guatemala City. Josan, the older of the two and I were getting something started. She of the dark eyes and the dazzling smile and three children from three different men, all by the age of twenty-six. Fortunately, I was talked out of it by John. Even for me, it was ridiculous.

I didn't like all the goddamn guns, either. One day an officer looked at me and our eyes locked. He stared at me with contempt and for some reason, I could not turn away. I saw all the perverse power he held and watched as his lips mumbled an obscenity. It struck me then it was time to look in another direction. I didn't travel thousands of miles to live in fear of a gun.

Not that Mexico is much different. When we crossed the Mexican border, Police came on the bus and rounded up the Guatemalans and shook them down. It happened a couple of more times, each time for a thousand or two thousand pesos. I guess this shit goes on everywhere, but some places are worse than others and on the whole, I would rather be in Mexico.

****

A day later entering Mexico City. For the last hour, we have been driving through the outskirts of the city. It seems to go on forever. There is something like twenty million people in Mexico City. It is difficult to comprehend, but as we drive through miles of shanties and then miles more of broken-down neighborhoods you get a numb feeling of what it might mean. It is a forbidding sensation, yet I know cities and am less afraid than if we were entering the countryside and look forward to experiencing this biggest of all cities. What's more, it is the center of Latin American writing and I wonder what secrets there might be. As we enter the taller buildings, I push back my fears and look straight ahead.

As things sometimes happen, in the hotel there is a person I met in San Blas. An older man named Jack from Australia who is a writer, no less. All this by chance in a city of twenty million people.

We have made an unspoken pact to hang out for a while. To see the different sights Mexico City has to offer and to share a beer together. You fall into these situations all the time when you're travelling. Brief encounters with another for two or three days before you part, never to meet again. It is strange and not the best way to handle human relationships, but the road is the drug we have chosen and it is not especially generous in this way.

Jack tells me his stories. When he worked on a sheep station in the Outback and separated sheep's guts. When he was a Beat in Melbourne. When he was married and was a journalist and had kids. Jobs in America, writing. People he met and places he has gone. His politics. His stomach problems from drinking too much. His regrets. The things that make him angry. The difference between Australian and American law and why he thinks American law is less fascist. I listen with a mixture of respect and pity and because he wants me to listen. This apparition of what I might be in twenty-year's time with the red nose and the stomach pains and the loose-fitting clothes and a big heart choked by life and too much feeling.

****

On the bus again. This time to a place called Guanajuato. A town hidden in the mountains two hundred miles north of Mexico City. It has been a month since I left the States. Juarez, Chihuahua, San Blas, Guadalajara, Oaxaca, Puerto Escondido, San Cristobal Las Casas, Lago de Atitlan, Mexico City and now, to a place called Guanajuato. They roll off my lips like far off destinations I have read about in a book, already vague and distant memories.

When I think of the Mexican people, a warm feeling comes over me. They have been in the background throughout the journey; kind, tender, soft people better than I. Brown hands wrapping tomatoes in newspaper, outstretched toward me. Directions to a street spoken slowly and with concern. A plate of tortillas set on the corner of the table with affection. The driver on a bus who calls me "Joven" and who looks after me in a paternal way, though I am older than he. Tears fill my eyes as we weave around the mountains and Guanajuato comes into view.

****

I am in San Miguel de Allende. I feel like an asshole, because I swore I wasn't going to live here. Guanajuato was nice, very nice, a magical town of different levels and winding passageways and garden plazas at the end of rambling, lost excursions. Something wasn't happening, though maybe I just felt lonely. Hell, Guanajuato could have worked out fine, but San Miguel hasn't been too bad, either.

Things have gone well. A lot of writing. I've got a room at a hotel for thirty bucks a week. In the morning, after I write, I go down to the Plaza and buy a newspaper and sit in the sun like the rest of the Gringos. Most of them are older and it reminds me of what Florida must be like.

Then I eat lunch and go play basketball with the local Mexicans. Even though the level of play is not very high, I struggle to keep up. They are ever so kind and generous. Always buying me a soda, each one shaking my hand as we part in different directions. After that I take a shower, get something to eat and try to crank out some more writing.

After dinner, I take a walk. Clear, cool nights with lots of stars and where you wear sweaters and scarves. I climb the cobblestone streets, up and down hills, resting at the top to look out in the distance. The city ends after a few blocks in any direction and there is nothing as far as you can see.

And then I walk back into town to my room and sleep for a few hours before the writing begins again.

****

I am on the road once more. Tomorrow morning, I leave San Miguel for a place called Zipolite. It happened a few hours ago. I was in a bar watching an American Football game and began talking to a young Mexican guy named Jose Maria. We got to talking about travelling when he said:

"I've travelled all over Europe and America and Canada. I know every place in Mexico, of course. I am Mexican, it is my country. The best place, the BEST place to have a good time, really nice people and cheap is: Zipolite. You can live there for nothing. Go to 'Gloria's' and tell them Jose Maria sent you."

The idea of spending a cold winter in Mexico didn't seem right. I should be at the ocean, playing in the sun, not holed up in some dark hotel room. Besides, San Miguel was starting to get to me. Too many would-be alcoholic poets and painters cornering you in a bar, telling you their tale. At times, for all its beauty, it seemed like a Gringo nightmare. Lost souls looking for something they can't find. I've been here three weeks, that's long enough. The Ocean calls. I'm getting the fuck out.

****

In Oaxaca for New Year's: home of the stumbling drunk. Never have I seen so many drunks stumbling down a street. I was sure they were going to fall on their face with their next step. They are amazing. Sometimes I stop and watch, laughing with disbelief. There is no way they can make it another ten feet, yet I have never seen one fall. I *have* seen a number lying in the gutter, however.

The drink of choice in Oaxaca is Mescal. Every block there are two or three Mescal parlors selling anything from a thimble to a gallon of Mescal and let me tell you, after a few thimbles of Mescal, you are flying. This American I met in one of the bars by the Plaza told me about his first New Year's in Oaxaca:

"I was living in a small town outside of Oaxaca and helped some of the people there and to thank me, they took me out for the New Year's celebration. We went to a party in Oaxaca and we were all drinking Mescal and the next thing I remember was lying in the street and people picking me up and taking me to a dark room and putting me on this big, soft, warm bed. It seemed like the softest bed I had ever been on in my life and I dropped off. I woke up, I don't know how many hours later and underneath me were ten or fifteen bodies, dead asleep."

****

WHAT AM I DOING? Walking down a dark, deserted beach in the middle of the night to someplace called "Gloria's." All I need is to get my ass robbed. I think I heard voices a little ways back. It probably won't happen, *but I am in Mexico.* If Gloria's is full, I'll have to walk all the way back down the beach with all my shit: money, passport, traveler's cheques. Yeah, I'd be fucked, alright. Nothing like a midnight stroll after an eleven-hour bus ride.

What a bus ride. Crowded, of course. There are never too many people on a Mexican bus. This one had the chickens and all. I had a comfortable seat on the floor at the back of the bus next to the screaming babies. All that was fine if I hadn't had the misfortune to sit next to a Jesus freak from Wisconsin for six hours. The kind who just found God and has come to Mexico to spread the word during his semester break, even though he doesn't speak a word of Spanish. Thought he'd warm up on me for a while.

I still can't believe it. From Oaxaca to Puerto Angel is one hundred and fifty kilometers, about a hundred miles and it took eleven hours. Up and down mountains. One minute freezing cold and the next sweating your balls off. Break downs and stalls and delays. I thought it would never end. After what seemed like forever, we arrived in Puerto Angel late at night. I didn't want to sleep there and after asking around, I finally convinced a taxi driver to take me to Zipolite. Ended up paying more for the taxi than I did for the bus! I am sure I got ripped off. The guy claimed the road was "*muy duro*" and would wreck his cab.

I got in the cab and he was right, the road was terrible and there was not a bit of light, the poor bastard sweating it out, banging his piece of shit cab all to hell. I felt like an asshole for giving him a hard time about the price. Finally, we got to the end of the line and he pointed to the beach. I walked down and asked around and as luck would have it, Gloria's was at the far end of the beach. It shouldn't be too much longer now.

****

Zipolite. This place is alright, I am staying at "Gloria's" except there is no Gloria here. She is on the lamb from the Mexican Authorities, or at least that is what I have been told. No one knows for sure, but she sounds like a real character.

Gloria has a nice set-up, by far the best in Zipolite. Most of the other places just have a couple of poles to string up your hammock and a thatched roof over your head, but at Gloria's we have actual huts with dirt floors. I live on the top tier and from my hammock I can look out over the Ocean.

There is the nude end of the beach and the other half of the beach where you have to wear a bathing suit. Guess what end I live at? Believe it or not, it is much calmer at this end. Nudists, in fact, are quite calm people. Being naked seems to take some of the aggression out of you, though I must confess I think about fucking all the time.

My day starts early with some writing. That is if I haven't partied too late the night before, or if there isn't someone in my hammock. That is a fairly big if, though I do try to get some writing in, before I rouse up my next-door neighbors, Kobi and Ronan and get something to eat. They are couple of Israeli guys who are in graduate programs in the States and who have befriended me.

After breakfast, we go body surfing for a couple of hours. Then we sit in the sun and talk, meet new arrivals and eventually, go to lunch. Food is surprisingly fresh and cheap. Salads and fresh fruit and seafood crepes. It is crazy. You don't even have to carry money. You just sign your name and settle-up at the end of the week.

Then it is time for a nap, a little reading, write a letter, play a game of chess and wait until the guys knock on my door to play volleyball at the other end of the beach with the Quebecois. They're all wrecked and within seconds there is a beer in my hand and a doobie in my mouth. We then get together and play volleyball until sunset. Where we then all take a swim in the Ocean, the sky full of colors. A shower, a fried fish dinner, some more beer and pot and then the walk to the other end of the beach and the end of another day. All for about fifty dollars a week. I probably won't be leaving right away.

****

It has now been over a month in Zipolite. When I go and where I go is uncertain. I am not terribly bothered. Life here is good. I have lived in rough places in my life, the wolf at my door, not knowing how I was going to pay rent or where my next meal was coming from. I accepted my fate and did my best to dig myself out of my unfortunate circumstances. Fate has now worked in my favor and why shouldn't I accept that as well?

Never have I had such a pleasurable existence. Sometimes I lie in my hammock and just laugh about it all. Whatever I need, whatever I want comes to me. The good meal, the swim in the ocean, the boyish camaraderie, the intellectual conversation, the exercise, the drug, the drink, the parties and of course, women. The less effort I make, the easier it is and I have stopped trying a long time ago.

Ronan and Kobi left a few weeks back and I have moved into their hut. It is bigger and has a bed as well as place to hang my hammock. No doors, only two openings in the front and back. A trail goes behind and through the front opening I can see the Ocean below as I lie in my hammock. Since I am up high, a cool breeze comes through at night. Small lizards crawl up the bamboo walls and plants grow on the dirt floor and nobody has taken anything from me, except a half bottle of mescal I used to clean my glasses. A few days ago, I turned thirty. A time to reflect and wonder what it all meant, if a wonderful French-Canadian woman named Danielle had not arrived at my door. We made tender, passionate love and my thoughts were swept away by the sensuality of our coming together. Forces greater than reason took hold of me and I surrendered once more. Nothing else mattered. Nothing else was so real and so good. Her flesh against mine, the sound of the night around us, meeting her lips to begin the fantastic adventure in front of us. Yeah, I'm happy.

****

It is time to leave Zipolite. I have been here for over two months and it is time to go. Like so many other people, I have stayed longer than I intended. Not many have stayed for two months, but Zipolite has been good to me.

Still no Gloria. I am now part of the woodwork, Armando getting me when he needs to explain something to new arrivals. Only the Quebecois are here from when I arrived: Gino and Ronald and George. Last year, they forgot one of their tribe. When they returned to Zipolite ten months later, he was still here.

I think of swimming in the ocean and how we catch waves after volleyball. A blue wall coming out of a red sky and how it catapults us to shore. Once I caught a tremendous wave, a wave you become part of and know your fate rests with the whims of the sea. It took me up, higher and higher, people shrinking below as I reached the crest. When I got to the top, I was motionless for a moment and then I was shot out as if from a cannon. I did my best to hold on. Behind me, I could feel a colossal force as I sped through the ocean. My body bounced on the water and I attempted to keep balance, until I relaxed for a split-second and the wave swept over me and my body was dragged underneath, turning over and over. I tried not to panic, telling myself the wave would be over before long. Long moments below until I was finally spit to the shore, the crown of my nose scraped and bleeding, my back mangled and sore and my bathing suit gone.

It is getting hot here. Almost too hot to even want to go swimming. I have been planning to leave for weeks, but I just can't seem to get it together. Maybe, I will figure out after a walk down the beach and a fish dinner. Or, maybe I won't.

****

And then it happens. Crow, Nanette and I are standing in the back of a truck as we leave Zipolite. I can see above the heads of the smaller Mexicans, dirt flying up as we bounce over potholes, Zipolite disappearing in the distance. On the road once again. We are headed to San Cristobal and after that, Palenque, the jungle ruins I have been waiting to see for so long.

Crow is called "Crow" because he looks like a crow. He has a long angular face with a hooked nose and a three-week beard. His hair is cut short and is balding on top and when he smiles, he has a few teeth missing. He looks like he has seen it all, which he seemingly has. Nanette doesn't necessarily look like a Nanette, but she fits perfectly with Crow She is not as weathered, though she does have a gold tooth, an experienced look beyond her years, long hair and a strong, wiry body. As does Crow, which he displayed in many a volleyball game.

They look like extras in "The Grapes of Wrath," wayward Okies travelling the roads of 1985. By comparison, I appear ridiculously young and unbothered, though I am only a few years younger than Crow and a year or two older than Nanette. I've slept in doorways and under freeways on occasion, but these guys are the real thing.

I think back to when Crow approached me a few days earlier about travelling with him and Nanette:

"Hey, Laddie, me and Nanette are thinkin' of leavin' in a couple of days and we were wonderin' if you wanted to come with us?"

I looked at him, touched by his offer:

"Where are you going?"

For moment Crow seemed lost, as if destination and direction were something he had never considered and shouted out:

"NORTH!…NORTH, MAN!" And he started to laugh. I shook my head and began laughing as well. Where else were you going to go from the bottom of Mexico? As the two and half months in Zipolite faded in the distance.

****

Waiting in Tuxtla Gutierrez for the 5 am bus to San Cristobal las Casas. The bus station is packed, people asleep on the ground. This is the third time I have been in Tuxtla. I haven't done anything but catch a bus here, but you never get out without a fucking hassle. We got here around 10 p.m. and, of course, just missed the last bus. We ended up crashing in one of the plazas in town and walked back to station at 4 a.m. in the morning.

The day was spent hitch-hiking and catching buses throughout a long, hot, dusty day. Most of Mexico is like that, a brown/gray landscape with an oppressive heat on the back of your neck. Stopping to get a taco and a beer in non-descript towns as you change buses. Almost all of northern and central Mexico is parched and brown and forever. Like one of those desolate landscapes in a Western where Clint Eastwood is riding into a limitless nothing, except since you're on a Mexican bus, he'll get there a couple of hours before you will.

But in the South, things start to come alive. Hills and ravines and rivers and jungles spring out of nowhere and everything Mexico wasn't is now on top of each other. Evergreen trees and twenty minutes later, a tropical forest, only to climb a mountain once again and see the Pacific Ocean in the distance. Your senses are flooded after miles of nothing and you sit back overwhelmed, unable to take it all in. I can't see going back up North.

30

****

Crow, Nanette and I have been in San Cristobal for a week. They love it here and it's been good hanging out together. Crow performs his juggling act, returning to the hotel with a hat full of coins. Nanette plays with little Indian girls, showing them how to knit and make toys out of newspaper. I write in the morning and we get a bite and something to drink later in the day.

The last four months, I've been pretty much a loner and Crow and Nanette have given me a sense of family for a while. The road can be tough. It only knows its own desires, the next destination along the way. From afar, it appears glamorous and it is in a lot of ways, but it can make you into a hard man. The continual leaving of places and people thickens your skin. All is forsaken for the next exotic locale and sentiment is pushed to the background.

I remember a fellow traveler who looked at me with frustration as I wrote postcards while we sat at a cafe. He could not understand. The need was gone. He had been around the world, but there was no longer anyone to write a postcard to, as he talked about Goa and Nepal and Bali and Machu Picchu.

Crow and Nanette have awakened old feelings. I realize how removed I have become. You learn how not to need anyone and that can become dangerous. They are much better than I at putting a human face on the road. I learn, but mostly I revel in our camaraderie. The three of us sitting down with a feeling of affection. Waiting for one or the other to pick up something at a store on the side of the road.

Allowing for vices that are not your own. Letting the white light rest for a while.

****

And then we are off to Palenque. Palenque are the Mayan Ruins set in the jungle of southern Mexico and Numero Uno on my list of places to see. When you travel, you hear about places, take Zipolite, I never heard of it until the night before I was on a bus to go there. It wasn't in any guidebook. But that's the way I like to travel, open to whatever sounds best along the way. I listen to the way people talk about a place and look at them, how they might compare to me. I don't know how many places I've gone, not knowing where I was headed, just because of the way it sounded. There is no place in Mexico that sounds so right as Palenque.

Of course, nothing in Mexico goes according to plan. We wake up early to make the 6 a.m. bus to Palenque, which arrives at 8 a.m. and is not only late, but is packed to the point of people standing in the aisles, which thirty more of us are supposed to fit, this on allegedly the single worst bus trip in Mexico: The infamous San Cristobal/Palenque Run.

The idea of standing up for eight to twelve hours with someone's elbow in my back, up and down hills, through the jungles of southern Mexico, unbearably hot and humid AND to have to actually pay as well, is too much for me. I yell back to Crow, who is behind me, jostling his way down the aisle: "Fuck this, man, I'm hitching!"

I work my way off the bus. A few moments Crow and Nanette get off as well. We cash-in our tickets and walk toward the main highway leading out of San Cristobal.

****

The hitch, like so many things in Mexico, is like a Dream. Surreal and its own and different from anything you have experienced before. We decide to split up, it will be easier that way to get rides. The going, for me, is slow. It takes me two hours to go thirty miles. I get a couple of rides, one on the back of a truck with some Mexican students. While we talk, an early morning wind blows through us. The rides take me only a short distance and I spend most of the time standing on the side of the road with my thumb out, until I see a bus which I flag down.

It is a local bus about to fall apart, full of Indians. They talk to me in pigeon-like Spanish and are full of kindness and patience. The bus travels to another world where everything is light green and a stillness in the air. Even when we stop and a crowd of people are around me, there is no shouting. This is how I travel until I get to a town called Ocampo.

Ocampo is high in the mountains with white-washed buildings, surrounded by a light haze. No one is on the streets and when I go into a store, the people are taken aback when I ask for a cake. I search out the bus station and find the next bus leaves in an hour and a half and decide to hitch until then.

I go down to the road and set my bag down and go in the bushes to take a piss when I hear wheels screech to a halt and voice yells out:

"Hey, Laddie!"

It's Crow and Nanette! I jump into the truck and I am introduced to a Mexican guy named Jamie. He works for the State of Chiapas and goes three times a week to …. *Palenque.*

For the next three hours, Jamie speeds through the jungle as we laugh about our good fortune. Green and Red and Blue and Brown fly past as we swerve the zig-zag roads towards our destination.

When we arrive in Palenque, Crow directs Jaime to a campsite next to the Ruins. There is an open-air shelter and we tie our hammocks to wooden stanchions, as the sun begins to set, the campgrounds empty beside the three of us. By the time we get in our hammocks, darkness sets and Crow tells us stories about his stay in Palenque five years earlier. He then talks about his busking, fiddler/juggler act. I have not known Crow to be much of a talker and it is interesting to see another side of him. I begin to drift off as Crow talks his way through his act, when a loud grunting comes up from the ravine below us:

"What the FUCK is that!?" I shout out.

"The Apes." Crow answers.

"The APES!?" I said.

"They won't bother us." Crow assured me.

The grunting is loud, reverberating in the ravine, near enough for an ape to climb into my hammock. Exhausted, I somehow am able to get to sleep.

****

Early, before light, I get ready for the day. I grab my flashlight and soap and shampoo and walk toward the showers. I remember the sounds of the apes and while it is unlikely, I am not absolutely sure there won't be an ape waiting form me in the shower.

I persevere and soon find myself under the cold water, washing away the grime of the last two days. In a short while, I will be in the pastures looking for mushrooms.

Whenever I trip, I go through a ritual of sorts. The right clothes: a pair of lime green pleated shorts with big pockets, a light blue T-shirt with a red sun and Acapulco written on front, a pair of rubber flip flops and a painter's cap. I stuff two thousand pesos in my back pocket and button it shut and I am ready. I want nothing extra on such adventures, nothing to lose. Experience has proven sparseness is the way to go. I may be cold for a while, but it will be a long day and most of it will be hot.

I leave the campgrounds and start walking toward the cow pastures in the dark. Crow told me you should go early because if you don't, the mushrooms get picked out. I like mushrooms. I like mushrooms a lot. They are my favorite drug and I always have a fantastic time when I take them.

I hear voices ahead of me. Americans. I introduce myself to a young couple from Vermont. Richard and Susan. He is a high school Science Teacher and she is a

Weaver. Together we go through the gates and enter the pastures as the sun creeps into the sky.

For over an hour, we look for mushrooms. Mud is splattered up to our knees and after a while we take off in different directions, scanning the ground, turning over cow patties. The mushrooms grow in cow manure. I have found only a few mushrooms, small, barely worth eating. Tired and dejected, I start walking back, looking for Richard and Susan. And then I hear Richard's voice:

"How'd you do?" Richard asks, calmly sitting on a log.

"Man, I didn't do worth a shit." I say, kicking the ground.

"We did pretty good." Richard replies.

He reaches behind his back and shows me a big plastic bag full of mushrooms, shiny and white.

I stand there, my mouth open, in disbelief.

It turns out while they were walking the fields, an Indian on a white horse came up to them and asked them if they wanted to buy mushrooms. The price they settled on was a thousand pesos for the bag. Richard and Susan are hesitant to eat them, but after buying some from them, I begin chomping away. The taste is not very good, like eating moist, bitter chalk, but I know where I am headed and eat them with glee. *And then, I am off.* The world becomes more intense, the colors brighter. I feel the sunshine on my face. An Indian on a horse on his way to work in the fields asks me: "*Te gusto los hongos?*"

I laugh and nod my head and ask him in Spanish how he knows about mushrooms. He returns my laughter and I feel myself kick off into a higher gear as we walk down a dirt path to the main road.

When we get there, who should be walking toward us, but Crow and Nanette! I introduce everyone, laughing the whole time and offer Crow and Nanette some mushrooms. Yes, they will take the adventure with me, or as Crow says with his usual aplomb: "Sure, Laddie."

Richard and Susan say they will meet up with us later and I bid them farewell. As Crow and Nanette and I walk toward the Ruins.

We walk down a paved road in the early morning sun when Crow goes into the bush. It's the "back way" Crow explains and we follow him out of the sun and down a moist dirt trail. He moves quickly and I struggle to keep up. My senses are flooded: the coolness of the jungle, the sound of running water, the moist ground beneath my feet, the smell of vegetation…*The Green.*

I plead for Crow to stop for a moment, but he tells me we will stop later and I find myself chasing after Nanette's bare feet as we scramble up the trail, over exposed tree roots, going higher and higher, until we are sitting on a ledge overlooking a waterfall, with rays of sunlight peeking through the trees and I have to hold myself back from jumping into it all.

We are back on the trail all too soon, as Crow speeds on. We climb higher and higher and reach a plateau and Crow cautions us: "There is a guard here. Just pretend you don't understand and keep on walking."

A guard appears and we follow Crow's instructions and everything works out just like he said it would. We walk along grass into the sunshine and Crow tells us we are entering the Ruins. I look around and see a few small, broken-down buildings and wonder: *Is this Palenque?*

I feel myself coming down, disappointed there is not more. Crow is studying hieroglyphics on one of the buildings. I feign interest, not wanting to believe this is all there is when Crow goes through an opening in a stone wall. I follow his lead and walk toward a stone bench in the distance and as I am about to sit down, I turn around and am surrounded by majestic temple pyramids reaching the sky.

From there, I go to yet another plane. The ground has been pulled from under me and I am on my hands and knees, helpless to what is before me. I shield my eyes, the brilliance, the enormity too great to handle. There is nothing left to do but surrender.

Feelings of submission overtake me as we begin to climb the steps of the Main Temple. Higher and higher we climb and I am transported to the days of the Mayan Empire. I am a pots and pans salesman on the way to peddle my goods to Royalty. Others walk past me unburdened, as I work out my sales pitch, scaling the steps on my hands and knees, my brass pots clanging away … It is all too much.

We climb and climb until my hand rests magically on the topmost step. I pull myself up and slide against one of the pillars and when I turn around and look out … *The horizon is a million miles away.* There is an endless ocean of green and at the end a clump of trees with low lying clouds. Once again, I turn my eyes away.

We sit atop the Temple, lost in our thoughts. Crow tells us how he lived in Palenque for two months, five years earlier. They had to literally cut the bindings of his hammock to get him out. Always had a chaw of mushrooms, sucked on them like an all-day lozenge.

"You can do some *thinking* here," Crows says with a distant look in his eyes.

I shake my head in astonishment, not even wanting to contemplate where I might be after two months on a magic mushroom diet in the middle of a Mayan jungle.

Of the rest of the trip, only flashes remain. The three of us watching in horror as busloads of American, German and Japanese tourists arrive. Scrambling up like ants, only to find us there, three sun drenched, half naked hippies with ridiculous smiles on our faces. Going down into the tombs and holding hands with an old lady from Minnesota, as I help guide her through the darkness.

Later swimming naked in the waterfalls, Crow telling us to watch out for thieves. Little tiny fish nibbling on our toes as we sit without talking in the jungle.

I separate from Crow and Nanette. I end up in town, dancing in a restaurant with local Palenque school children in costumes as they solicit money for a new hospital, salsa music blaring away.

Going back to the Ruins. Back through the waterfalls. Meeting various strange folk, the more normal, the seemingly more bizarre. Running through the temples with a woman named Cas. We are stopped by a guard in a belfry who asks us for our tickets. I can't seem to find mine. I search my pockets, not wanting to pull out the bag of mushrooms, the plastic crackling all too noticeably, the guard asking me what I have in my pocket, *"Lo que esta en su bolsillo?"* Telling him it is not his job to ask me what is inside my pocket. The tension building as I search for my ticket, trying to keep my composure, as I answer his questions in Spanish, until, finally, I find my ticket. We walk past him and out of the temple as the sun sets on the jungle.

Coming down from the trip, back at the campgrounds, lying in my hammock. Crow talking about his juggling act, the best towns to make money. Nanette telling me about their days on the road and how it has gotten better. Falling asleep to the sounds of the jungle and Crow and Nanette's road tales.

Waking up early to take the train to Mexico City. In our care, an Italian mushroom casualty whose friends ask if we can drop him off at the Italian Embassy. He is wearing dress pants and a white collared, button-down shirt and is barefoot and penniless with no papers.

A thirty-hour train ride in a second-class car, where you are afraid to go to sleep for fear of waking up without your possessions. A young thief taking Cas' Walkman right off her lap. We all watched in amazement as she chased him down the aisle, screaming and swearing, the young thief jumping off the slow-moving train and through the yard and out of sight.

The next day, the long, slow haul to Mexico City. Until, at last, we arrive at our destination and I am hugging Crow and Nanette good-bye. I watch them disappear as I walk toward the bus to Sand Miguel.

****

Back in San Miguel. The Plaza is crowded with tourists and the weather is warmer than when I was last here. A few hours to kill before I take the bus back to Mexico City. I arrived yesterday evening and saw a friend who was keeping a few odds and ends for me: books, old letters, scraps of clothes. He is originally from Texas and is an aspiring writer and supports himself and his two children by selling condominiums in the resort areas of Mexico. Unable to find a hotel room, I end up sleeping on the floor of his apartment, the kids giggling and excited by a stranger being in their home. I drop off amidst their father's remonstrations and their shrieks of laughter in the dark.

In the morning, I go to pick up my mail at the post office. Before I left, I made provisions for my mail to be held and I am anticipating a backlog of letters from the last three months. When I get there, I am told most of my mail has been sent back. I lose control and start screaming in Spanish and English, gesturing madly, not wanting to believe after having filled out numerous forms and paying money to ensure my mail being held, almost all of it has been sent back to the States. But then I realize nothing is going to bring back those letters, I am in Mexico, after all. You must accept the show you have paid for and if my mail had been there, it wouldn't be Mexico. I leave with the few letters that weren't sent back, shaking my head, stunned, angry, filled with loneliness and dismay.

I head toward the Plaza where I buy a cup of strawberries and cream from a vendor and sit on a curb. A man comes up to me. A painter with loose fitting white clothes, holding canvases. He has a New York accent and starts to come on to me. He asks how I like my strawberries, what a wonderful day it is. I look up at him with a bored expression, letting him know I am aware of his intensions and am totally uninterested.

To which he responds, shouting bitterly:

"The Mexicans have an expression: Lost Gueros son putas!" And storms off.

I stare into my strawberries and cream and realized I gave the vendor a thousand peso note, instead of a hundred peso note and feel another knife stab me in the chest. I grab my bags and walk toward the bus station, shaking my head.

****

A few days in Mexico City. This is my third or fourth time in Mexico City and I wonder how many more times I will end up here on my trip. It is like a whirlpool, dragging me into its vortex anytime I am near. Here, they call it simply: *Mexico.* The place is overwhelming. I still know little about this gargantuan city, what it means, the significance of it all. Forever expanding, tens of thousands of people arriving daily. Defying logic or common sense or the poverty of the millions upon millions already here. The fate of which rests on the throw of the dice.

I have found a place near the main zocalo. A room I reach via a winding staircase with wooden floors and French windows and three beds and where I can hear the prostitutes yelling at night. Sometimes I sit on the balcony watching the street life below and wonder where this is all taking me. Or aimlessly roam the avenues in this cavernous city before finally trudging up the stairs and entering my room with a skeleton key.

Down the road is the Palace of the Governors. Inside, is Diego Rivera's: "History of Mexico," a collection of murals depicting Mexico's past. They are incredible and I can look at them for hours, only to come back the next day and start all over again. I wonder why I haven't heard more about this man. I have seen all the big painters in Europe and if this guy isn't right in the thick of it, then I don't know fuck about Art. Perhaps, his art is too confronting. Fantastically powerful canvases beyond the parameters of timid minds. Every civilization is up its own asshole and recognizing Diego Rivera would be like giving matches to an arsonist. You either surrender or look the other way.

****

And then, I am in Tuxtla, yet again, at the bus station, waiting in line to buy a ticket. Even if I do get a ticket, it won't be for the next bus and I wonder how long I might be in Tuxtla this time. As I wait in line, I see some Mexicans talking to a cab driver. They are bargaining with him for a price to San Cristobal and seeing my chance, I get out of line and stand near them. Twenty-five hundred pesos for the lot, which with me, makes five hundred pesos a head. We get a couple of more guys and make it four hundred pesos a piece, plus a little more for the driver. We then pile in, I up front, smashed in the middle and off we go to Las Casas.

The drive is beautiful. The view in a car is different from a bus and I notice things I haven't noticed before. We are closer to the ground and soon it is one long scenic postcard. There is little conversation. Mexicans tend to be simple, not particularly inquisitive people and no one asks me where I am from. There are a few words stating the obvious, that I am going to San Cristobal, how pretty it is, and then there is silence. And before long, one of the men is against me asleep. Then, the other. Within a few minutes, the whole car is snoring away except for me and the driver. We go up and down the mountains with their heads back and mouths open all the way to San Cristobal. I get off at the Plaza and carry my bags to a hotel down a cobblestone street as the sun sets on this town, I have chosen to spend the next three months.

****

I live outside the main town of San Cristobal at a campground called: Rancho San Nicolas. When Crow, Nanette and I were here, someone mentioned it and I went for a look. There are nine or ten cabins set on a hillside, though most of them are nothing more than shacks. It is away from the cafe scene in town and will be good for writing and it is as beautiful as you could want. My shack is on the top tier and from my porch I can see all of San Cristobal. The whitewashed buildings set in the green mountains with the two big churches on either side of the town.

The surprise is how cold it gets at night. It gets fucking cold! I can't believe I was complaining about how hot it was a couple of weeks ago and I am now shivering away every night in my hammock. The days are fine, in fact, the sun can be almost too bright on clear days About five or six, a chill creeps in and I prepare for the night. I get stoned at the same time and it's hilarious putting on sweatpants and sweaters, pretty much my whole wardrobe, until I am in my trench coat and hat and scarf, watching the sun set on Las Casas. As the stars litter the sky and fireworks are set off in town, my high making it all right.

I go to bed early and wake up in the middle of the night, the wind howling outside my walls. There are no other sounds and I light a couple of candles and start writing away. The book could be good, but New York, all the people I knew, seem so far away. Sometimes I find myself talking to them, laughing at old conversations we once had. The objective is to keep writing and not worry about it. Novels are not written overnight. You see the story in your mind and what is on paper rarely matches your vision and you tell yourself that's what rewrites are for. All the time knowing it must be better than anything you have ever done before. There is more to it than talking to pretty girls about D.H. Lawrence over espressos.

Eventually, I have written all I can and fall asleep. I wake up when it is still dark and go down to the kitchen and make breakfast. No one else is up and I make oatmeal and toast and take it up to my cabin. I eat in silence and think of the task before me, telling myself to keep going, every day of writing brings my dream closer to realization. The problem is I am not at the point where I can see the light at the end of the tunnel and it is impossible to be sure of anything at all. Faith carries the day, though sometimes it doesn't. You don't want to see things too clearly with this stuff. Reality is as much a danger as delusion.

****

My life in San Cristobal has settled into routine. There are still places to see, but I have seen enough on this trip. Time is running out and soon I will be back in the States making rent. What is left, the next three months or so, I must devote to writing. Hole myself up in my little shack and get into it.

Every other day, I go into town to the market to buy groceries: tomatoes, avocados, mangos, bananas, onions, cucumbers, oranges, bread and cheese. The market in San Cristobal is famous and you can understand why, the colors are magnificent and the produce ridiculously cheap and fresh. Avocados five or ten cents each. Three large mangos for thirty cents. Throughout the market are the local Indian tribes. They are like the Indians in Guatemala and come to the market in their own distinctive dress. There are at least five or six different tribes in San Cristobal and they come to the market each day to sell their produce and goods. Where I live, I pass Indians to and from town. They greet me with their shy smiles and luminous eyes and I smile back and say: "*Buenas Dias*." Their way of life, their trusting of fate is something I don't have. There is a happiness all too real and I feel vulnerable in the face of it.

The other day, I watched a father flying a kite with his young son. The joy in their eyes, their amazement with what the wind could do with a bit of paper and sticks. It wasn't any moral instruction endeavor, any means to an end father and son outing. The father was having as much fun as the child and they both reveled in their joy. They laughed when the kite took off into the sky and they laughed when the wind died down and the kite crashed and fell to the earth, running across open fields to retrieve it and bring it to flight once more. I sat down on the side of the road and watched with my eyes filled with tears.

****

I have a friend, a street dog who has adopted me as a companion and who hangs out at my shack. He is only a puppy, really. A young, small to medium sized dog with a short, light brown coat and a muscular build. As far as I can tell, he doesn't belong to anyone. He roams around the campsite and the neighboring houses getting by as best he can. In a country where the people don't eat all that well, it is a challenge, but he seems to make out, alright. He's crafty and quick. If he wasn't, he wouldn't have lasted. I've named him Nick, after the campground, Rancho San Nicholas.

He finds me at the end of my breakfast and when I clap my hands, he races up the hill at a breakneck clip. I give him the pot with whatever oatmeal is left and he has it spotless in no time. Any other scraps I have he eats as well: old mangos, bananas, carrots, avocados, potatoes and bread. He gives anything a try, which is smart because I don't baby him. I will be gone one day and I don't want him relying on me too much.

Nick began to come around more often and before I knew it, he expected three meals a day. Whining and whimpering, grabbing my pants' cuffs with his teeth, scratching at my door if I was inside. The son of a bitch even went above my shack, kicking stones onto the roof and waking me up during naps!

I let Nick know that he would eat at *my* convenience. That he was to be happy with what I gave him, that I called the shots, but Nick has a full bag of tricks. He is quite the actor, a regular Lawrence Olivier of the canine world. Things came to a head one afternoon when I was reading on my porch. First the whining began, which I have gotten used to. He then grabbed at my pants' leg and when that didn't work, he started eating the grass, grazing as real as any cow. I looked at him impressed, but figured if it was good for cows, it probably was not too bad for dogs either.

I went back to reading until I heard a crunching noise – *the bastard was eating my shack!* I couldn't believe it at first, but Nick was diligently chewing on the side of my shack. I got up and gave him a good kick. Nick moved away from the shack and then charged me with his teeth bared. We fought back and forth for a few moments, until I picked up a rock and Nick seeing my hand raised, fled down the hill, the rock just missing him as he tore down the hill and out of the campground.

He came back a few days later apologetic and full of remorse. I missed him. We pretended nothing happened, though I gave him a talk, a while later. He understood (My opinion of canine intelligence has gone way up since meeting Nick) and things have gone fine since then. I wasn't so different myself when I was his age. A street kid using bluff and con and guile to get what I wanted. I understand why he is the way he is, but I don't want to be treated as a mark. Hell, Nick is the best friend I've got.

****

I have been in San Cristobal a month and it is still cold. Last night, shivering away in my hammock, I wondered what it was all about. Certainly not freezing my ass off on top of some mountain. Is this where I want to be at thirty?

These fucking cold nights are getting the better of me. Not getting any mail doesn't help. I'm not going to lie, it's been hard. I've been away before, but I don't think I've ever been this alone.

I think of a woman who I once loved and who loved me as well and wonder if we could start again. Why not? If she's willing to take a chance, I am too. I am not too crazy about living in Boston, but hell, I could live anywhere for a year. What's all this chasing my tail around the world for anyway? Doesn't love count for anything? To be with a woman who loves you, understands and knows who you are, and who you love as well, is that a bag of shit? Even if I had everything, would I not still want that?

She's probably got a boyfriend. She might even be married. All I can do is send my feelings to her and whatever happens I can accept. If she is happy then I am, no matter the circumstances. I know she loves me and that alone has carried me on many a dark night. But might she want me? Didn't she call me last summer and told me she loved me? Was that an illusion, or did that actually happen? … No, that happened, I'm sure it did. I will write her tomorrow and then it is up to her.

****

On the way to town today I realized I am not going to finish the book during my time in Mexico. It's April and I've got a long way to go, hell, I've only just begun. The more I do, the more it unravels. I'll have to go back to Santa Fe, work like a demon and then take off for somewhere and hopefully, finish it off. Probably, somewhere in Asia.

When I go to the market, Nick is beside me until we reach the cobblestone streets, before turning back. His turf is the area around the campgrounds. Sometimes from my porch, I see him sniffing around the nearby houses. I put a collar on him I found the other day. Not to claim him or anything, just so people think twice before shooting him, or making him into the special of the day.

I am sure I have eaten dog since I have been in Mexico. It wasn't beef. Since then, I always order chicken The other day I was at a restaurant with friends. Every few minutes we heard the sound of a dog, yelping for his life, coming out of the kitchen. It went on and on, until, finally a guy stood up and said: "OK, who ordered steak?"

The place roared with laughter.

Going to town isn't all fun and games these days. There is a Local who hangs out at the cafes who hates me. He is a tall European Mexican named Angel. He has a dangerous reputation and I have no idea what he has against me. We have tense stare downs and it has gotten where I am ready for a fight when I go to town. The good news is it keeps me from hanging out all day in the cafes.

I have made a friend in town. An older Mexican man who runs a small leather shop near the market. I drop in on my way to shopping and we talk for a while. He offers me an orange or banana and we laugh about our day. How he rides his bicycle and takes a swim on Sundays. I tell him about the different places I have visited in Mexico.

He is a little guy, but he has a lot of energy and is proud of his work. His leather is softer and thinner than the other shops and after a while, you can fold your bag in half and then, again. This far down in Mexico it is impossible to get cheated, you will never pay half what you would pay in the States, but even in San Cristobal, my friend's work is a good deal. I have brought a number of new customers into his shop. And then I am on my way back to the cabin. My bag bursting with fruit and vegetables as I walk the cobblestone streets to the edge of town.

Sometimes there are Indians selling produce on a street corner. The Indians selling here are poor and they could use the money, but they aren't above ripping off a tourist and I always ask the price before I buy anything. After that, it is the long dirt road to the campground. By the time I reach my shack, I am sweating and tired and Nick is jumping up and down around me.

The nights are cold, colder than when Crow and Nanette were here two months ago. The weather is starting to get my spirits down and I am thinking of going to the coast for a week or so. In a couple of months, the rainy season starts. All you do all day is sit and watch the rain fall.

****

Yesterday I went to San Juan, one of the Indian villages outside of San Cristobal. It is the home of the Chamulas, one of the Indian tribes in the area. The church in San Juan is a landmark and I have been told is not to be missed. You follow a path on the outskirts of town. The trip takes two hours, most of it uphill.

As I was walking up the hill, Indians passed me walking to and from the market. You should see the legs on these guys. I thought about writing a short story about one of them becoming a champion marathon runner, running barefoot and in his native costume. Hard to imagine doing this five times a week, loaded down with goods, barefoot and cold.

The Chamulas have a reputation of being aggressive and can be very pushing while making a sale. They are the least liked of the tribes for that reason. Many a day, I have been in the Plaza reading the paper and have been bothered by a Chamula trying to sell me an artifact or trinket. There is just so much shit you can buy.

But I didn't come to San Juan to buy souvenirs. The Church here is supposed be something completely different and soon I have a fifty-peso entry ticket in my hand. From the outside, it looks normal enough. Inside, though, it is dark, except for the flickering of candles throughout the Church. All the pews have been removed and straw is on the floor. Small groups of Indians gather around various alters and appear to be praying and chanting. When I get closer, however, I notice most of them are completely off their face, blind drunk. Many of them are passed out and asleep on the floor. They seem to be drinking a clear liquid out of Pepsi bottles. Some form of Mescal, no doubt.

After the initial shock, I walk around. The Church strikes me as more sensible than most of the churches I have seen. There is no priest or leader, not set order. Everyone seems to be practicing religion in a way they feel most comfortable. The Church feels like a sanctuary, a place you can go without feeling self-conscious. I walk toward the front and painted on the ceiling are lions and tigers and panthers in bright, surreal colors and with strange expressions on their faces. I gaze up and feel myself being swept away.

****

Last night was so cold I could not write. I woke up in the middle of the night as usual, but it was so cold I could not concentrate on writing, the wind blowing through the thin walls of my shack. I couldn't get to sleep either, even with a hat and scarf. I assumed by April in Mexico, Southern Mexico, no less, this would not be the case.

After breakfast, I prepare for a week-long trip to the Coast. There is a place called Puerto Arista and after packing my bag, I say goodbye to Nick and my friends at the Campground and walk to the outskirts of town. The hitching isn't especially good, but I keep moving. A straight ride takes four hours, I am hoping to make it to Puerto Arista by nightfall.

It is the Easter holiday. The cars that pick me up are Mexican families on their way to see relatives. They are in a festive mood and offer me beer and shots of whiskey. Twice I get invited to spend Easter with people I just met. It all goes easy and soon we are driving into Puerto Arista at about 4 pm. Another beer, a dance with the wife of the last guy I got a ride with, warm goodbyes and I am by myself and need to find a place to stay.

Puerto Arista is packed with people and after an hour of looking, I realize there isn't a room to be had in the entire place. Panic sets in, but then it fades; I am a little drunk and far too tired to worry. Not a physical tiredness as much as a nervous exhaustion. I go to a beach bar and order a beer and something to eat. The people are kind and I rest my bag against my leg. If I sleep on the beach, so be it. I can't pull a room out of my ass.

Before long, I find myself with a group of young Mexican guys. We are drinking beer and laughing. They sense I am on my own and pull me into their group. They all work together and many of them play on the local soccer team in Oaxaca. The songs start and each one of them sings a song, until it is my turn to sing. They urge me on, clapping their hands, patting me on the back and I end up singing a Motown song: "My Girl" by The Temptations. They all clap and want me to sing another and I sing: "My Cherie Amour" by Stevie Wonder. The last song I sing is: "Yesterday" by the Beatles, which most of them know, or at least can hum to. By the end of the song, we are all clapping.

The next couple of nights I spend drinking beer and swimming and going out to the local discos with my new-made friends. Puerto Arista is bursting with people for the Easter holiday, thousands upon thousands of tourists, hundreds sleeping on the beach. As far as I can see, there are nothing but Mexicans. I look for other foreigners, but there aren't any to be found. As the weekend winds down, tourists start to leave. My friends depart as well, giving me their addresses and a blue "Cruz Azul" soccer shirt. By Monday, there aren't a hundred tourists in all of Puerto Alvarado. With all the people gone, it will be a good place to get some writing done.

****

As active as the weekend was, during the week is that dead. By Wednesday, I am the only guest where I am staying. The days are long and hot and boring. I work on the book and read "One Hundred Years of Solitude" by Gabriel Garcia Marquez in slow, ten-page chunks. The family running the place are very nice, simple rural folk and I talk to the younger sons for a while each day. But mostly I sip on a beer, take long walks on the beach and eat the specialty and only item on the menu: big, deep fried, battered prawns.

One day, I go for a swim around sunset. The waves are big and I decide to go body surfing. A group of Mexicans watch, cheering me on, amazed at what I am doing. Of course, these are people who swim in a pair of pants and shirt or wearing a dress. By the time I finish, there is a crowd of nearly a hundred people surrounding me. I am handed a glass of beer and asked question after question about who I am and where I am from. One man wants me to go to a place called: *Tres Picos.* He has two daughters who smile at me and he asks me to pick one or the other, or both. He tells me how beautiful Tres Pecos is and I am tempted, but realize the ridiculousness of the scenario and beg off, claiming I am married and have a wife to return to in the States. We say goodbye, laughing, strange hands patting me on the back as I walk back to my room, shaking my head. Mexico. The only place I am considered marriage material.

The remainder of the week drags by like a novel, only more monotonous. Writer in Mexico at a secluded beach town with the sounds of roosters, clanging dishes and the constant gibbering of Spanish in the background. I tell myself this is part of the movie as I stare at the walls of my room.

Then, there is a knock. The guy who runs the place wants to know if I have any "*Revistas Desnudas.*" I tell him I do not have any naked magazines, but then he sees my copy of "One Hundred Years of Solitude" with a drawing of a man and a woman in a naked embrace. He becomes excited, but is let down when there are no naked photographs. He asks me what the women are like in America and raises his hand above his head and says, excitedly: "*Muy Alta con piernas grandes, blancas, gordas!*"

I laugh hysterically, visualizing seven-foot women with big, fat, white legs. I tell him the women in the United States are more or less the same but can tell he is determined to keep his fantasies and don't press him.

I go to take a swim and notice the Ocean is very turbulent. The waves are big and breaking irregularly and you feel in danger before you go very far out. To my side is a woman. I move closer to her and soon we are talking. She is an American from, of all places, Chicago, where I grew up. The waves are crashing around us and then we are in embrace, running our hands over each other's bodies, kissing passionately. We go on like this for five or ten minutes, the Ocean tossing us back and forth. Until we decide to get out of the water and I see, as we are walking along the beach, this woman I have been in a lustful encounter is over six feet tall with big, long white legs. I look around to see if anyone is watching.

****

On the bus from Tuxtla to San Cristobal where I spent the last three days with the Tall Woman. These bends in the road are becoming the staple of my existence. Ah, but I'm only human. I need to feel the warmth of another body, the touch of a lover, no matter how fleeting. A slip of paper is given to you with an address and a phone number and you follow it.

I left Puerto Arista on hot, steamy morning and caught a crowded taxi into town. Sleepy eyed men and a fat woman holding a chicken on her lap, as the wind cooled us as we raced down the road. The moment we stopped, the heat enveloped us. I sluggishly walked to the bus station and though Tuxtla was a three-hour bus ride away, it was after dark when I got there. Most of the day, spent waiting for buses, slapping flies, fighting off the heat.

Once I arrived in Tuxtla, it was another adventure. More buses, more directions asked, more confusion, until finally, I am walking down a deserted street with my bags after midnight toward an address of a woman I spent an hour on a beach with four days earlier. We kiss each other on the cheek. I take a shower and moments later, we are making love under a mosquito net, the sound of bugs outside the window, drowning out our moans. Looking up at the ceiling as my hand rests on her shoulder as she sleeps.

****

On my way back to San Cristobal, I think of another woman. I wonder if a letter has come from Alessandra. I find myself writing to her as we head toward the mountains. I am taken to her embrace, her stare, her kiss. The trip to San Cristobal cannot go fast enough, but when I get there and go to the post office, there is no letter and I find myself taking the long walk down the cobblestone streets to the campground, my head down most of the way.

Life at the campground resumes as if I never left. I am surprised how many people I know, even if only on a "*buenos dias*" level. Nick isn't there when I arrive, but when he sees me a couple of hours later, he takes off like a bullet and is all over me for a half hour. He's grown some. He'll never be big, but he's gotten a little bigger and thicker. He's game, too. He'll mix it up with dogs a lot larger than he is. The poor bastard has probably seen more life than I ever will.

There is a young Mexican woman named Rosa with two small children who lives next to me. She is from up North and speaks English well and I have thought about getting involved with her, but it would be a mess. I have no idea where I will be in six months, Europe, Asia, Australia, who knows? Better off being her friend.

It's hard being a single, divorced woman in Mexico, especially this far South. I try to keep her spirits up and babysit the kids when she needs to go into town. They're good kids, a boy, Eric, four years old and Gabby, who is about a year and a half younger. She is going to be something else. She climbs the hill to my cabin like a mountain goat and isn't afraid of anything.

Three times a week, I go running with Guerillmo, a Guatemalan refugee now living in San Cristobal. He is short and muscular with a beard and glasses and runs me into the ground. We take the road out of town, going higher and higher into the mountains. I feel myself getting fatigued and just try to forget. All I see is Guerillmo's stocky body in front of me. Up and down the hills, until we enter the backside of town. Running down the cobblestone streets, children cheering us on. Up steep flights of stone stairs and back down, again, passing the churches and small shops. Finally, down to the valley and we are sprinting down the dirt road to the campground. I collapse on the grass and sit in the shade until I can summon the courage to walk up to my shack.

****

Less than a month to go before I head back to the States. I am getting excited and even think about going early. Hell, half the time my mind is in America, anyway. It's like that when you travel. You find yourself continually projecting to the next destination, undermining the experience where you are. Already, I am planning out possible scenarios when I get back to Santa Fe. San Cristobal is becoming less real. My visions of the future cloud my senses to the degree where what is in front of me seems like an illusion.

There are moments I am not in Mexico at all. Physically, I am here, but I am filing it all away like postcards for some later date. I've seen more different sights and sounds than any trip I can remember, but it's been hard on me. Too fast and abrupt and jarring. I am not a particularly good traveler. I find myself getting involved, attached. The human element gets in the way. This is not just some detached adventure to log away or put in a scrapbook. I am not a Mexican, yet this country will stay with me from now on. Not just those parts I want to keep, but those things which this country is, both beautiful and hard.

I don't have a camera, which is stupid, considering all the places I have been. For some reason, it seems like a violation. I rather bathe in my memories, experience a moment, and let it sink in. In my mind, I take a picture, a picture with smells and textures and sounds and moods and feelings. If I train my mind, I won't need a camera, I tell myself. I can sit on my porch for hours, lost in reveries, my life coming back to me like a super alive movie. Memories flooding over me like a soft, warm wave.

Before I leave Mexico, there is one last place I want to go: Agua Azul, the jungle waterfalls about a hundred miles from here. I have left Agua Azul for last, a going away present to myself. In a couple of weeks I will make the trip, return for a week or two and head North. Until then, I keep my head down and make as much headway with the writing as I can.

****

Still no word from Alessandra. I wonder if she even *got* my letter. You never know with this fucking Mexican Postal service. I am right next to the United States and there is a 50/50 chance of my mail getting in and out of the country. Un-fuckingbelievable.

At times, I almost hope the letter hasn't arrived. Already, I have visions of Asia and the South Pacific in my mind. If I work my ass off this summer in Santa Fe, I could be gone in September. Sure, I would love to be with Alessandra, nobody has gotten me like she has. But she has been more elusive than something I can hold. She loves me and she must know I love her as well, but what does that mean? Letters and phone calls out of the blue declaring her love, only to find her gone when I reach out. And me, all over the place, chasing my mad visions. Would I be able to hear her message, anyway?

After a day's writing, I'll get stoned and have conversations about it all. The idea of living in Boston in the winter doesn't exactly appeal to me. I have never been there, nor have I had a desire to go, but a lot of people I respect rave about the place. And I wouldn't be going to Boston to go Boston, anyway. I would go there to be with Alessandra, to have our relationship be at the center of my life. Scary stuff and I am not all sure it's what I'll want in six months, but I'm willing to give it a try.

So, I'll go back to the post office tomorrow and hope there is a letter from Alessandra. I've gotten letters, so I know some people are getting my mail. Life will be good, whatever happens, In Boston with Alessandra, or on an island in the South Pacific writing the book. There are things bigger than one's wishes and desires and you must accept that truth. .... I am getting more Mexican by the day.

****

I have finally arrived at Agua Azul. Not without complications, of course. The bus I was on ended up fifteen miles past Agua Azul and I had to wait two hours for another bus to get me back to where I had been three hours earlier. It wasn't the driver's fault, but the son of a bitch taking the tickets. He fell asleep and when he woke up, Agua Azul was long gone.

I asked the guy if we had gotten to Agua Azul yet and he waved me off like I was an idiot child. Forty minutes later, he was running down the aisle to get me, bleary eyed and panic stricken. I was tempted to ask for my money back, but grabbed my bag, gave him a dirty look and thanked him with sarcasm: "*Gracias para todo, Amigo!*" … Makes the experience more authentic, I suppose. It was almost worth it to see the look on the bastard's face as he was running down the aisle.

The Waterfalls are two or three miles from the main road and it's not exactly hiking weather. I am dripping with sweat and am hoping I won't be disappointed, but Mexico doesn't get the best public relations. I have seen amazing things here I never heard about when I was in the States. I just need to keep a good pace and I will be there before too long. At least, I know there is a nice swim waiting for me at the end of the line.

****

We have finally found the Lost Waterfall. For three days I have been swimming the waters of Agua Azul with two Australians, a Dane, an American and a German woman in search of a mythic waterfall. A Niagara Falls in the middle of a sleepy jungle. They had been searching for the waterfall for three days before I joined them. On the sixth day, we found it. It is magnificent. A colossal sheet of white water appearing out of nowhere.

The adventure was like something out of Tarzan movie. A series of waterfalls in the middle of the jungle lasting five kilometers. The six of us leaving our hammocks in the morning and diving into the water. The bluest water you will ever see, so blue it is turquoise, as turquoise as any stone. Swimming into the jungle, moving along the banks of the river and diving off a waterfall to get to the next level. Hitting the water and feeling your body pulled under.

Down, down, until you are spit up and you are swimming toward the next waterfall. The noise of the jungle filling your ears. Purple, red, orange flowers exploding with color on low hanging trees. Exotic birds hovering above your head. All the time moving forward on a turquoise path … *We went on like this for hours on end.*

We were about to give up when we heard this sound. In the distance you could hear this WHOOSHH and we knew we were getting closer. We swam toward the sound and it seemed to disappear, only to come back stronger than ever. On we went, our ears alert to the sound of the Waterfall. We could feel it somewhere out there. Until finally, it was there in front of us. This gigantic sheet of turquoise water crashing down in front of us, the sound deafening.

These things don't come naturally to me. I am a city boy and not a particularly good swimmer. There is always a moment of hesitation and indecision when I am confronted by nature. Not like these Australians, who dive into it all like taking a coin out of their pocket. No fear, no thought, no pause, just go for it, but I am not too far behind. My blood begins to surge and my stomach starts to flutter. I can feel myself losing control. I am no longer my own master. As I sit on a rock in the sun, hypnotized by the Waterfall, its' spray covering my body.

****

And then I am on my way home. It is mid-May and I am preparing to leave the campground, the final pack and I am saying good-bye to Nick. I look in his eyes and try to communicate my feelings. He has a few new scratches on his face. A fight, no doubt and I wonder how long he'll survive. I give him my lecture on life: "Don't fuck around too much. Be cool. It's tough out there, etc." But then I realize how ridiculous it all is and how even if he could understand me, he'd know all these things. I look at him once more, tell him I love him and that we'll always be friends and head down the hill.

I stop at Rosa's place and give her food, pots and pans and a thousand pesos for the kids. We hug and she has tears in her eyes. I give her words of encouragement, but stop myself from wondering how she will get by and walk over to Guillermo's cabin. I give him some clothes, including a double-breasted blazer. I roll up the sleeves so it will fit him, cursing him one last time for running me into the ground. We laugh and shake hands and I walk out of the campground and down the dirt road, Nick following me for a while before turning back.

I am not sorry about leaving. I am ready to go. *Mexico.* It has been a humbling experience. I want to go somewhere where my illusions can run. Too much of what I once thought has been undermined. Not in a dramatic way, but chipped away, bit by bit, until I am left with no ground beneath me. These damn Indians. Like my old friend and town said: "*Los Indios son mejor.*"

Sure, the Indians are better, but where does that leave me? Like a dude I met on a bus from New York who was living in the mountains with Indians for the last four years. *He was way the fuck out there.* An errand boy for a tribe, a million miles from where he came. He didn't seem especially happy, but I could understand. And while I understood, I didn't want to go where he was. No, take my ass back to America.

****

A few days in town staying at a hotel in San Cristobal. The two Australians, Craig and John, as well as Steve, the American are here. We'll hang out for a couple of days and Craig and John will head to Guatemala and Steve and I will head North. It will be the last bus I will take for a while.

The bus to Mexico City will be long, but I don't mind. In fact, when Steve suggested we take the bus rather than the bargain flight from Tuxtla, I was quick to agree. How else could you leave Mexico *but* by bus? Twenty-four hours on a bus sounds cruel, though then you think: "It'll be dark soon and I will go to sleep. I'll wake up, read a little, talk with Steve, take a nap and we'll be there."

San Cristobal already feels distant. The hotel room, the last three days, pulling stuff out of my bags. Sitting at the bus station, I felt San Cristobal leave me. My mind is going to another place.

Travelling with Steve will be good preparation for coming back to America. Everyone has a plan, a schedule, a timetable, a formula. He is full of ambitions and strategies, though he is only twenty-six. I listen to him, amazed how anyone so young can be so driven, until I am become bored with all his empire building and say: "Enough of the bullshit, for a while, O.K., Steve?"

I forget how much Americans reveal their lives to one another. It is like everyone is practicing for when they become rich enough to afford a therapist. Steve reveals it all. Not just his tycoon plans, his ventures into real estate, his plan to open up a cabaret club, his ambition to be a singer, his relationship with alcoholic, abusive father, his homosexual double life, his trauma of being overweight as a child, the occasional thickness of tongue when he speaks, the rejection of a recent lover. This from someone from Austin, Texas I have known for less than a week. I suppose I should be grateful I am not with a New Yorker, or someone from California.

Steve gave a rendition of his nightclub act one evening in Agua Azul, complete with taped background music. It was hilarious. Not because he wasn't any good, I am sure Steve was the most professional performer Agua Azul has seen in years, but because as soon as he started to sing, it began to pour down with rain. We were under an aluminum roof and it sounded like the end of the world.

We moved closer and closer to Steve, but the closer we got, the harder the rain came down. Until were sitting right in front of him and all we could hear was the deafening jungle rain. Steve slogged on, determined not to let anything like a jungle monsoon stop the show. The sight of him singing his lungs out, doing all his schmaltzy, Las Vegas routines and the five of us hunched over at his feet, unable to hear a word, was priceless.

The sun is setting on San Cristobal for the last time. It grows smaller in the distance as Steve tells me what it feels like to be an overweight kid in Texas and not like football. I nod my head and feel my eyes grow heavy, darkness enveloping the bus. I drop off to Steve's words fading in my ear.

In Mexico City. We are staying with Diego, a friend of Steve's, for a few days. He is a fashion designer and lives in a big house in one of Mexico City's nicer neighborhoods, complete with maid, sunny garden and modern amenities.

After a shower and meal, we are off to party. Everyone is connected to the fashion industry: models, photographers, fashion designers and agents. They are dressed in stylish outfits and talk about the most recent episodes of American television shows "Dallas" and "Dynasty."

Everyone appears to be gay, including a couple of American models who are in demand for their Anglo appearance. There is also Dominique, the French model who lives with Diego. She walks around the house in short shorts and cut off T-shirts and takes my breath away every time she passes by.

Having lived in New York City and San Francisco much of the last seven or eight years, it is oddly familiar. Like a wave of nostalgia sweeping over me with a Spanish accent. Laughter and martinis and marijuana for a few final days before heading home.

The fashion industry, like every other industry in Mexico, is rife with racism. It is controlled by European Mexicans and the image of beauty is blatantly European. The last time I was in Mexico City, I was struck by billboards with European faces and blond hair and how perverse it was. I had been in Zipolite for nearly three months and was very dark and could not find anyone lighter than me out of thousands of people rushing past me on at the Metro station. Films, television and magazines are dominated by European Mexicans, even though they make up a fraction of the population. As I am handed another martini and lose myself in gibberish about television soap operas.

****

The last two or three days have passed like an erotic dream. Most of it has been spent in Dominique's bed, wrapping our bodies around each other. We were sitting and talking one night when she put her head on my shoulder. I stroked her neck and ran my hand down her back. She took my hand and off we went. Kissing, falling on her bed in the dark, knowing we were on the verge of something extraordinary. Our clothes falling away, our naked bodies rubbing against each other. We were on our way.

To look into another's eyes and know they will run. Run as far as you and then take you further out to sea. Our bodies pulled along on a sensual carpet toward something greater and more alive. Where we go of no concern, only the going. As I lift her legs and lick her body. And she climbs my back and bites my ear.

Long talks into the night. We are not so unalike. Two wayward souls travelling the world, without any preconceived plan, following the direction most real, until we end up in Mexico City in each other's arms. She has lived a full, varied life, but senses, like me, that all knowledge and all experiences are to be pushed aside when a chance for magic is to be had.

What else matters? To be a child, naked to the experience and let it take you. To be moved by your heart and not question, but only follow. Our reward falling on top of us like a velvet waterfall as we are taken to a higher place.

I look into Dominique's eyes and see the certainty of these things. My arms falling around her body until my hands are touching her thin taut waist, reaching lower till my fingers run the crack of her ass. She pressing down on me, stretching out her arms, kissing me on the neck, as one dance leads into another. Our words stop only for other words to begin. Sensations on top of sensations as we go deeper into our adventure. Tumbling into night, holding hands as the stars shine through the window.

****

The last days in Mexico are spent in the Immigration Office getting my visa straightened out. I have overstayed my visa and have made up a story of losing my papers while my hotel was burglarized. No big deal. There are not a lot of Americans trying to sneak into Mexico, but the Mexican bureaucracy lived up to its reputation. I would have offered a bribe if I knew how, but instead played it straight for fear of getting into trouble. Two long days for something that should have taken five minutes. I finally get out at 4 p.m. on a Friday and have two hours to get back to Diego's and take a shower and pack my bags.

Getting anywhere in Mexico City is a challenge, especially on a Friday at rush hour. Forget a cab. Islands in the middle of the street are packed with people hailing cabs and after waving frantically for five minutes, I figure it is best to take the Metro to the outskirts of town and try my luck there.

I descend stairs and am met by a human ocean and wait patiently as the crowd is systematically pushed into cars. Twenty minutes later, I am jammed into my last subway car in Mexico, surrounded by all too familiar sights. Whole families moving to other parts of the city with bags around their feet. Vendors selling chewing gum and cigarette lighters. Students. Office workers. Victims. I am sweating, holding onto a pole with a lost look in my eyes, waiting for the last stop.

When we get to the last stop, we all charge out and scramble up the stairs. It is raining outside and the buses to the outer part of the city are besieged with passengers. I head toward the taxi islands, which also have thousands of more passengers than they can take. I get at the end of a long line, the rain falling on top of me.

The whole scene is mad. The slowly moving line, until once more I am pushed into a crowded car, people on top of me, eight of us in a cab. We head off creaking and groaning toward the expressway, the traffic bumper to bumper. Somehow, I get to Diego's house on time. In truth, I don't even know how I got there. I ring the bell and Eva, the maid, opens the door. Dominique is behind her and I walk to where she is standing.

I kiss Dominique good-bye as a taxi waits to take Steve and I to the bus station. She is in a blue gauze sarong and a sleeveless blouse showing a brave face. What is there to say? I tell her she is an amazing woman and to not let anyone tell her differently. I can feel her love and affection roll on top of me. Her arms are around me and she is silently looking into my eyes. There is no need for words Finally, I break away, walk toward the taxi, turn around and kiss her one last time and head out the door. She is in the doorway as the taxi takes off.

I suppose I could have stayed. Diego and Dominque said I could make money as a model, that my look would work. But I can't stay in Mexico, as a model in Mexico City, no less. I have all but proposed to another woman. Even though there is a chance she has not received my letters. Or, that I never got hers.

No, I have to leave. Even if there wasn't another woman, or job waiting for me in Santa Fe. I need to get on familiar ground for a while. In a few months I may be off again, but I have to catch my breath. I am exhausted.

****

When Steve and I are on the bus, all I can think about what it will be like on the other side of the border. It's already dark, Steve is sitting in the aisle seat, like a buffer as we move toward Nuevo Laredo. It will be only minutes before I am asleep. When I wake in the morning, we will be a few hours from America. The events of the last few days, my anticipation of what is to come, fade away. I lean my head against the window and drift off to sleep.

I wake up several times during the night. The sound of Spanish spoken in earnest, of babies crying and old grandmothers attempting to soothe their fears. I listen as if for the first time. Their goodness and humility pierce my heart. They want so little. Only a life a little more comfortable, some work, each other. I wonder why it is so much more difficult for them to achieve this than for others, than for me. I fall asleep, hoping they get the things they want.

Then it is morning and we are driving the last miles to the border. The ugly, dreary Northern Mexican landscape, the shitty little towns. The last hundred miles seem to last forever. We stop at every outpost along the way. My patience wears thin and my nerves are on edge. The weather is heating up and I can feel the humidity.

But, then, we are 'there.' We are filing off the bus, grabbing our luggage from the side of the bus. Steve has arranged for a friend to pick us up and we wait in a bus station reeking of every smell from enchiladas to urine to whisky. Families are hunched over their belongings. The station filled with drunks, hustlers, deadbeats and people selling sunglasses and combs.

The Border Patrol policeman suspiciously goes through my bags. He finds my journals and asks what they are. I tell him I am writing a book. He opens a journal and begins to read. I see his eyes move up and down the page and the expression on his face turn to disgust. He closes the journal, opens it again and begins to read once more and then shoves it in my bag, shaking his head. He waves me on as I walk laughing toward America.

****

The ride to Austin is along rolling, green plains, the landscape manicured and antiseptic. Every now and then a store or strip mall appears painfully clean with shiny new cars in the parking lot. We stop at a store with a banner saying: "We Sell 'Texas-Style' BBQ Ribs & Chicken" and soon I am buying ribs from a suburban cowboy with a white hat and starched blue jeans and belt with a big silver buckle. He is friendly, loud and distrustful and seems like he is from another planet. We return to the car and head toward Austin. As I eat my "Texas-Style" ribs, the adventure begins anew.

****

"Mexico" was written in 1987, in a third-floor apartment in Sydney, Australia overlooking the Pacific Ocean, the lone building left on a condemned block in downtown Bondi Beach. It was an account of my nine-month journey to Mexico undertaken in 1984-85. By the fall of 1988, I was in New York City, hawking my second book, which "Mexico" was the largest offering in a collection of stories.

More than thirty years later, I am offering "Mexico" once more. I am now an old man, where I was once a young man. I have renamed the story: "Lost in Mexico: Journey into an Exotic Land." It remains, in my opinion, the best writing I have ever done. For some reason, the story seems more timely than ever.

I see "Lost in Mexico: Journey into an Exotic Land" in the pockets of Mexicans in Mexico City and in countless other cities and towns throughout the Mexican landscape. It is a foreigner's homage to their amazing, complex, beautiful country I was once fortunate enough to experience.

Lenny Jacobson

Project Name Lost in Mexico: Journey into an Exotic Land

09.04.20XX

—

Your Name
Your Company
123 Your Street
Your City, ST 12345

Overview

Lorem ipsum dolor sit amet, consectetuer adipiscing elit, sed diam nonummy nibh euismod tincidunt ut laoreet dolore magna aliquam erat volutpat. Ut wisi enim ad minim veniam, quis nostrud exerci tation ullamcorper.

Goals

1. Lorem ipsum dolor sit amet, consectetuer adipiscing elit.
2. Sed diam nonummy nibh euismod tincidunt ut laoreet dolore magna aliquam erat volutpat.

Specifications

Nam liber tempor cum soluta nobis eleifend option congue nihil imperdiet doming id quod mazim placerat facer possim assum. Typi non habent claritatem insitam; est usus legentis in iis qui facit eorum claritatem. Investigationes demonstraverunt lectores legere me lius quod ii legunt saepius.

Lorem Ipsum

Duis autem vel eum iriure dolor in hendrerit in vulputate velit esse molestie consequat, vel illum dolore eu feugiat nulla facilisis at vero eros et accumsan.

Milestones

I. Lorem ipsum

Lorem ipsum dolor sit amet, consectetuer adipiscing elit, sed diam nonummy nibh euismod tincidunt ut laoreet dolore magna aliquam erat volutpat.

II.   Dolor sit amet

Lorem ipsum dolor sit amet, consectetuer adipiscing elit, sed diam nonummy nibh euismod tincidunt ut laoreet dolore magna aliquam erat volutpat.

www.ingramcontent.com/pod-product-compliance
Lightning Source LLC
Chambersburg PA
CBHW061759050726
47598CB00002B/791